Saltwater Savvy: The Ultimate Guide to Setting Up and Maintaining a Thriving Reef Tank

Chapter 1: Introduction to saltwater fish tanks

- Definition of saltwater fish tanks
- History of saltwater fish tanks
- The benefits of keeping a saltwater tank
- Different types of saltwater fish tanks (e.g. fish-only, reef, FOWLR)

Chapter 2: Setting up a saltwater fish tank

- Choosing the right size tank for your space and fish
- Equipment and supplies needed for a saltwater tank (e.g. heater, filter, substrate, lighting)
- Setting up and cycling the tank

Chapter 3: Choosing the right fish for your tank

- Compatibility of different fish species
- Factors to consider when choosing fish (e.g. size, temperament, care requirements)

- Recommended fish for beginner saltwater tank hobbyists

Chapter 4: Filtration and water quality in a saltwater tank

- The importance of good water quality
- Different types of filtration systems (e.g. mechanical, chemical, biological)
- How to test and maintain water quality

Chapter 5: Feeding and nutrition for saltwater fish

- Different types of fish food (e.g. flakes, pellets, live/frozen)
- How much and how often to feed saltwater fish
- Supplementing with vitamins and minerals

Chapter 6: Common health problems in saltwater fish and how to prevent them

- Symptoms of common saltwater fish diseases (e.g. white spot, velvet)
- How to prevent and treat fish diseases
- The importance of quarantine for new fish

Chapter 7: Reef tanks: an introduction

- What is a reef tank and why keep one
- The difference between a reef tank and a fish-only tank
- The benefits and challenges of keeping a reef tank

Chapter 8: Setting up and maintaining a reef tank

- Choosing the right size and equipment for a reef tank
- Setting up and cycling a reef tank
- Maintaining water quality in a reef tank

Chapter 9: Choosing and caring for invertebrates in a reef tank

- Different types of invertebrates suitable for reef tanks (e.g. coral, anemones, shrimp)
- Compatibility of different invertebrates
- Feeding and caring for invertebrates

Chapter 10: Common health problems in reef tanks and how to treat them

- Symptoms of common invertebrate diseases (e.g. coral bleaching, velvet)

- How to prevent and treat invertebrate diseases
- The importance of quarantine for new invertebrates

Chapter 11: Advanced techniques for experienced saltwater tank hobbyists

- Advanced filtration systems (e.g. protein skimmers, ozone generators)
- Advanced lighting systems (e.g. LED, T5)
- Advanced water movement systems (e.g. wavemakers, current generators)

Chapter 12: Conclusion: the joys and rewards of keeping a saltwater tank

- The personal and educational benefits of keeping a saltwater tank
- The importance of conservation and responsible hobbyism
- Tips for continuing to learn and grow as a saltwater tank hobbyist

Chapter 1: Introduction to saltwater fish tanks

Saltwater fish tanks, also known as marine aquariums, are specialized systems designed to house and maintain a variety of saltwater creatures. These tanks can range in size from small desktop setups to large, custom-built installations.

The history of saltwater fish tanks dates back to the mid-19th century, when the first marine aquariums were established in public aquariums and zoos. However, it was not until the 1950s and 60s that the technology and knowledge for keeping marine fish in home aquariums became widely available. Today, saltwater fish tanks are a popular hobby for people of all ages, with a dedicated community of enthusiasts sharing tips, advice, and experiences.

There are many benefits to keeping a saltwater fish tank. In addition to being visually pleasing, marine aquariums can provide a sense of relaxation and stress relief. They can also serve as a learning opportunity, teaching hobbyists about the biology and behavior of different marine species.

There are several different types of saltwater fish tanks to choose from, depending on the interests and goals of the hobbyist. Fish-only tanks, also known as FO tanks, are the most basic type and contain only fish, with no live coral or invertebrates. FOWLR tanks, or fish-only with live rock, contain a mix of fish and live rock, which provides a natural habitat and helps with filtration. Reef tanks, on the other hand, are more advanced and contain a variety of coral, invertebrates, and fish, creating a miniature ecosystem.

Chapter 2: Setting up a saltwater fish tank

Setting up a saltwater fish tank requires careful planning and attention to detail. The process involves choosing the right size tank for your space and fish, selecting the necessary equipment and supplies, and properly cycling the tank before introducing any fish.

When choosing the size of your tank, it's important to consider both the space you have available and the needs of the fish you plan to keep. As a general rule, bigger is better, as larger tanks are easier to maintain and provide more stable conditions for the fish. However, it's important to also consider the size and growth potential of the specific fish species you plan to keep, as well as any other equipment or decorations you might want to include in the tank.

There are several pieces of equipment and supplies that are essential for a saltwater fish tank. These include a tank, a stand or cabinet to hold the tank, a heater to maintain a consistent water temperature, a filter to remove impurities and maintain water quality, and a substrate (e.g. sand or gravel) to provide a natural-looking base for the tank. Depending on the type of tank you are setting up (e.g. fish-only vs. reef), you may also need additional equipment such as a protein skimmer or lighting specifically designed for coral growth.

Once you have all the necessary equipment and supplies, it's important to properly set up and cycle the tank before introducing any fish. The process of cycling a tank involves establishing a balance of beneficial bacteria that will help to break down waste and maintain water quality. This can be done through a process called fishless cycling, where a source of ammonia is introduced to the tank and the bacteria are allowed to grow and establish themselves. Alternatively, you can cycle the tank with a small number of hardy fish, but this method can be more stressful for the fish and requires careful monitoring to ensure their health.

Chapter 3: Choosing the right fish for your tank

One of the most exciting parts of setting up a saltwater fish tank is choosing the fish to include in it. There are hundreds of different species of saltwater fish to choose from, each with its own unique characteristics and care requirements.

It's important to research and carefully consider the compatibility of different fish species before making any decisions. Some fish are more aggressive and may not do well with more docile species, while others may have specific dietary or habitat requirements that need to be taken into account. It's also a good idea to avoid mixing fish from different regions, as they may have different water temperature and pH requirements.

There are several factors to consider when choosing fish for your tank. These include the size of the fish (both at adult size and as a juvenile), the temperament of the species, and the care requirements of the fish. Some species are more sensitive or require more specialized care, which may not be suitable for beginner hobbyists. It's also a good idea to consider the ultimate size of the fish and whether it will fit comfortably in your tank as it grows.

For beginner saltwater tank hobbyists, it's often recommended to start with hardy fish species that are easier to care for and less sensitive to water quality and other environmental factors. Some examples of hardy fish for beginners include damselfish, blennies, and gobies. As you gain experience and confidence, you can consider adding more delicate or specialized species to your tank.

Chapter 4: Filtration and water quality in a saltwater tank

Maintaining good water quality is essential for the health and well-being of the fish and other inhabitants of a saltwater tank. Filtration systems play a key role in removing impurities and maintaining water quality, and there are several different types to choose from.

Mechanical filtration involves the use of filters or filter media to remove physical debris and waste from the water. This can include items such as uneaten food, fish excrement, and excess algae. Mechanical filtration is typically achieved through the use of a filter sock or pad, which removes larger particles from the water as it passes through.

Chemical filtration involves the use of chemicals or chemical media to remove impurities from the water. This can include activated carbon, which removes dissolved organic compounds and discoloration, or zeolite, which removes excess ammonia.

Biological filtration is the process of establishing a balance of beneficial bacteria in the tank that helps to break down waste products and maintain water quality. This can be achieved through the use of live rock or a specialized biological filter media.

It's important to regularly test and maintain water quality in a saltwater tank to ensure the health and well-being of the fish and other inhabitants. This can be done through the use of test kits to measure parameters such as pH, ammonia, nitrite, and nitrate. Water changes should also be regularly performed to remove excess waste and replenish essential elements.

Chapter 5: Feeding and nutrition for saltwater fish

Proper feeding and nutrition is essential for the health and well-being of saltwater fish. There are several different types of fish food available, each with its own set of benefits and considerations.

Flake food is a type of dehydrated fish food that is readily available and easy to store. It is typically made from a variety of ingredients, including fish meal, plant matter, and vitamins and minerals. Flake food is suitable for a wide range of saltwater fish, but it is important to choose a high-quality brand and to avoid overfeeding.

Pellet food is another type of dehydrated fish food that is made from a similar range of ingredients as flake food. It is available in different sizes and is suitable for both small and large fish. Pellet food is generally more nutritionally complete than flake food, but it can be more expensive and may not be as readily accepted by some fish.

Live or frozen food is another option for feeding saltwater fish. Live food, such as brine shrimp or black worms, can provide a natural source of nutrition and can be particularly useful for finicky eaters or for conditioning fish for breeding. Frozen food, such as bloodworms or Mysis shrimp, is a convenient alternative to live food and can be thawed and fed as needed.

In addition to providing a varied diet, it's important to also consider the frequency and amount of feeding for saltwater fish. Overfeeding can lead to excess waste and poor water quality, while underfeeding can lead to malnutrition and stunted growth. It's generally recommended to feed small amounts of food two to three times per day, rather than a single large feeding. Supplementing with vitamins and minerals can also help to ensure that the fish are receiving a balanced diet.

Chapter 6: Common health problems in saltwater fish and how to prevent them

Saltwater fish, like any other animals, can be susceptible to various health problems. It's important to be aware of the signs and symptoms of common diseases and to take steps to prevent them from occurring.

One common disease in saltwater fish is white spot, also known as Ich or Ichthyophthirius multifiliis. This is a parasite that can cause white spots to appear on the skin and fins of the fish. White spot can be caused by poor water quality, stress, or a compromised immune system. It is typically treated with a combination of medication and improved water quality.

Another common disease is velvet, also known as Oodinium. This is a parasite that causes a golden-brown or rust-colored film to appear on the skin and fins of the fish. Velvet can be transmitted through water or through contact with infected fish, and it is often more severe in younger or weaker fish. It is typically treated with medication and improved water quality.

There are several steps that can be taken to prevent the occurrence of diseases in a saltwater tank. These include maintaining good water quality, providing a varied and nutritionally complete diet, and avoiding overcrowding. It is also important to quarantine new fish before introducing them to the tank to ensure that they are not carrying any diseases. This can be done through the use of a separate quarantine tank or by using a hospital tank within the main tank. Quarantine allows any potential diseases to be detected and treated before they can be transmitted to the rest of the tank inhabitants.

Chapter 7: Reef tanks: an introduction

A reef tank is a specialized type of saltwater tank that is designed to replicate a miniature coral reef ecosystem. These tanks are more advanced and require a higher level of commitment and care compared to traditional fish-only tanks.

One of the main differences between a reef tank and a fish-only tank is the presence of live coral and invertebrates. Coral, which is actually a type of animal, provides a natural habitat for the fish and helps to maintain water quality through the process of photosynthesis. Invertebrates, such as anemones and shrimp, add additional biological diversity and can serve as a food source for some fish.

There are several reasons why someone might choose to set up a reef tank. In addition to the visual appeal of a miniature coral reef, these tanks can provide a sense of relaxation and can be educational, teaching hobbyists about the biology and behavior of different coral and invertebrate species. However, it's important to note that keeping a reef tank is a significant commitment and requires a higher level of care and attention compared to a fish-only tank.

There are several challenges to consider when setting up and maintaining a reef tank. These include the need for specialized lighting and filtration systems, the need to carefully control water quality and parameters, and the potential for coral and invertebrates to contract diseases. However, with proper planning and care, a reef tank can be a rewarding and enjoyable hobby for experienced saltwater tank enthusiasts.

Chapter 8: Setting up and maintaining a reef tank

Setting up and maintaining a reef tank requires careful planning and attention to detail. There are several factors to consider when setting up a reef tank, including the size and type of tank, the type of lighting and filtration systems, and the selection of coral and invertebrates.

When choosing the size and type of tank for a reef setup, it's important to consider the size and growth potential of the coral and invertebrates you plan to keep, as well as the number and size of the fish. A larger tank will provide more stable conditions and allow for more flexibility in terms of the types of coral and invertebrates you can keep. It's also important to consider the type of lighting and filtration systems that will be needed to support the coral and invertebrates.

Lighting is a critical factor in a reef tank, as coral and some invertebrates require specific wavelengths and intensities of light to survive and thrive. The most common types of lighting for reef tanks are metal halide and LED, with each having its own set of benefits and considerations. It's important to research the specific lighting requirements of the coral and invertebrates you plan to keep and to choose the appropriate lighting system accordingly.

Filtration is another important aspect of a reef tank. In addition to the mechanical and chemical filtration provided by a traditional fish-only tank, a reef tank may also require a protein skimmer to remove excess proteins and other organic matter from the water. It's also important to regularly test and maintain water quality in a reef tank, as even small changes in parameters such as pH and temperature can have a significant impact on the health of the coral and invertebrates.

Maintaining a reef tank requires a regular schedule of feeding, water changes, and equipment maintenance. It's important to research and follow the specific care requirements of the coral and invertebrates you have in your tank, and to be prepared to adapt to any changes in the tank's conditions. With proper care and attention, a reef tank can be a rewarding and enjoyable hobby for experienced saltwater tank enthusiasts.

Chapter 9: Choosing and caring for invertebrates in a reef tank

In addition to fish, coral, and live rock, a reef tank can also include a variety of invertebrates, such as anemones, shrimp, and crabs. These creatures add additional biological diversity and can serve as a food source for some fish. However, it's important to carefully research and consider the compatibility and care requirements of different invertebrates before adding them to your tank.

There are several types of invertebrates that are suitable for reef tanks. Coral, which is actually a type of animal, provides a natural habitat for the fish and helps to maintain water quality through the process of photosynthesis. There are many different types of coral available, each with its own specific lighting and care requirements. Anemones are another popular invertebrate for reef tanks, and they can provide a home for clownfish and other symbiotic species. Shrimp, crabs, and other invertebrates can also be added to a reef tank, but it's important to research their specific care requirements and to ensure that they are compatible with the other inhabitants of the tank.

Invertebrates, like any other animals, have specific care requirements and can be susceptible to diseases. It's important to research and follow the specific care instructions for the invertebrates you have in your tank, including their feeding and nutrition needs. It's also important to monitor the health of the invertebrates and to be prepared to take action if any problems arise. This can include quarantining new invertebrates, treating any diseases that may occur, and making any necessary adjustments to the tank's conditions. With proper care and attention, invertebrates can be a valuable and enjoyable addition to a reef tank.

Coral is an essential part of a reef tank, providing a natural habitat for the fish and helping to maintain water quality through the process of photosynthesis. There are many different types of coral available, each with its own specific lighting and care requirements. It's important to carefully research and consider the compatibility and care requirements of different coral species before adding them to your tank.

One of the main considerations when choosing coral for a reef tank is the type of lighting it requires. Different coral species have different lighting requirements, and it's important to match the lighting in your tank to the needs of the coral. Metal halide and LED lighting are the most common types of lighting for reef tanks, and it's important to choose the appropriate system based on the specific needs of the coral.

In addition to lighting, there are several other factors to consider when caring for coral in a reef tank. These include water quality, water flow, and feeding. It's important to maintain good water quality and to keep the water parameters within the desired range for the coral. Water flow, which can be achieved through the use of a wavemaker or powerhead, is also important for coral health, as it helps to distribute nutrients and remove waste products. Some coral species also require supplemental feeding, either through the use of specialized food or through the addition of small amounts of natural or frozen foods.

Coral, like any other animals, can be susceptible to diseases. It's important to monitor the health of the coral and to be prepared to take action if any problems arise. This can include quarantining new coral, treating any diseases that may occur, and making any necessary adjustments to the tank's conditions. With proper care and attention, coral can be a valuable and enjoyable addition to a reef tank.

Chapter 10: Common health problems in reef tanks and how to treat them

Like any other animals, coral and invertebrates in a reef tank can be susceptible to various health problems. It's important to be aware of the signs and symptoms of common diseases and to take steps to prevent them from occurring.

One common health problem in reef tanks is coral bleaching, which occurs when the coral expels its symbiotic algae, causing it to turn white. This can be caused by a variety of factors, including high temperatures, low pH, or high levels of light. Coral bleaching is typically reversible if the cause can be identified and corrected, but it can lead to the death of the coral if left untreated.

Another common problem in reef tanks is the presence of nuisance algae, which can compete with the coral for space and nutrients. Nuisance algae can be caused by a variety of factors, including high nutrient levels, improper lighting, or the presence of excess nutrients in the water. The use of algae-eating invertebrates, such as snails and herbivorous fish, can help to control nuisance algae, but it's important to address the underlying cause to prevent it from recurring.

There are several steps that can be taken to prevent the occurrence of diseases in a reef tank. These include maintaining good water quality, providing the appropriate lighting and water flow for the coral and invertebrates, and avoiding overcrowding. It is also important to quarantine new coral and invertebrates before introducing them to the tank to ensure that they are not carrying any diseases. This can be done through the use of a separate quarantine tank or by using a hospital tank within the main tank. Quarantine allows any potential diseases to be detected and treated before they can be transmitted to the rest of the tank inhabitants.

If a disease does occur in a reef tank, it's important to take action as quickly as possible to treat it and prevent it from spreading. This may involve the use of medication, such as antibiotics or antiparasitics, and making any necessary adjustments to the tank's conditions. It's also important to carefully follow the instructions for any medication used and to monitor the health of the coral and invertebrates during treatment.

In addition to preventing and treating diseases, it's also important to practice good husbandry in a reef tank to maintain the overall health and well-being of the coral and invertebrates. This can include regularly cleaning the tank and equipment, performing water changes, and providing a nutritionally complete diet. By following these steps and being proactive in the care of a reef tank, it is possible to maintain a healthy and thriving miniature coral reef ecosystem.

Chapter 11: Advanced techniques for experienced saltwater tank hobbyists

As a saltwater tank hobbyist becomes more experienced, there are several advanced techniques that can be explored to take the care of their tank to the next level. These techniques can help to create a more realistic and dynamic environment for the fish and other inhabitants of the tank, and can provide additional challenges and rewards for the hobbyist.

One advanced technique is the use of a refugium, which is a separate compartment or tank that is connected to the main tank. A refugium can serve several purposes, including providing a space for macroalgae to grow, which helps to remove excess nutrients from the water and can provide a food source for some invertebrates. A refugium can also provide a space for copepods and other small invertebrates to breed, which can serve as a natural food source for the fish in the main tank.

Another advanced technique is the use of a calcium reactor, which is a device that helps to maintain the proper levels of calcium and other elements in the water. Calcium is an important element for the growth and health of coral, and a calcium reactor can help to provide a consistent and stable supply.

There are also several advanced techniques that can be used to replicate specific environments or habitats in a saltwater tank. This can include creating a mangrove forest or a seagrass bed, which can provide a more realistic and dynamic environment for the fish and other inhabitants.

By exploring these advanced techniques, experienced saltwater tank hobbyists can take their tank to the next level and create a more realistic and dynamic ecosystem for their fish and other inhabitants.

Chapter 12: Conclusion: the joys and rewards of keeping a saltwater tank

Keeping a saltwater tank can be a rewarding and enjoyable hobby that provides a sense of relaxation and connection to the natural world. It allows hobbyists to create and maintain a miniature ecosystem, filled with a variety of colorful and interesting fish and other inhabitants.

In addition to the visual appeal of a well-maintained saltwater tank, there are several other joys and rewards that come with this hobby. These can include the opportunity to learn about the biology and behavior of different fish and invertebrates, the sense of accomplishment that comes with successfully caring for and maintaining a tank, and the opportunity to create a relaxing and peaceful environment in one's own home.

While keeping a saltwater tank does require a commitment of time and resources, the rewards of this hobby can far outweigh the challenges. With proper planning and care, a saltwater tank can be a source of enjoyment and relaxation for many years to come.

Printed in Great Britain
by Amazon